A WORLD LESS PERFECT FOR DYING IN

by

Ralph Pennel

Červená Barva Press
Somerville, Massachusetts

Červená Barva Press
P.O. Box 44037
W. Somerville, MA 02144-3222

www.cervenabarvapress.com
editor@cervenabarvapress.com

Visit the Bookstore at: www.thelostbookshelf.com

Cover art: "Rising Tide" by Resa Blatman

Author photo: Shelly Mosman

ISBN: 978-0-9861111-7-4

Library of Congress Control Number: 2015940835

Distribution: Small Press Distribution

ACKNOWLEDGMENTS

Thanks to the publications in which the following poems have appeared:

Unbound Press, "Planning Our Departure"; *Up, Up and Away: A SASE Wings Anthology,* "Camera Shy"; *The Smoking Poet,* "On Looking at A Photo of Two Soldiers on the Wall in Costello's Bar, Saint Paul" and "Just off the Hennepin Bridge"; *The Waterhouse Review,* "Shooster"; *Muddy River Poetry Review,* "Elegy to Young Boys Jumping off the End of the Dock"; *Istanbul Literary Review,* "Comprehensive List of What the Earth Owes Me for My Time Here So Far"; *The Somerville News,* "Confiding in the Prison Guard"; *Wilderness House Literary Review,* "Under the Missing and Innumerable Stars" and "To Have and to Hold" and "All That Remains"; *The Bagel Bards Anthology,* "Elegy to the Heart and all that It Endures"; *Right Hand Pointing,* "Three Girls Talking About Love"; *Ibbetson Street,* "My Father's Son, My Brother" and "Nighthawks"; *Open to Interpretation,* "Tomorrow, and Tomorrow, and Tomorrow"; *Apercus Quarterly,* "Watching the Sandhill Migration, First Light Easter Morning, in Nebraska's Platte River Valley"; *The Cape Rock,* "What We've Come to Expect from Beauty" and "Jesus Was A Handsome Man"; *Ropes,* "Endurance"; *The Four Quarters Magazine,* "Premonitions of an Early Retirement" and "Free This Poem. It Wants to Fly" and "Because We Were Assigned to Write Bad Fiction" and "The Deaf Couple Their Fight and the Healing Hands of Angels" and "Photo Taken of Me Atop the World Trade Center, November, 1995"; *Ibbetson Street,* "A Nearly True Poem about Postcards from the MOMA She Never Knew She Wanted Until Today"; *Ibbetson Street,* "Proving Grounds"

TABLE OF CONTENTS

Notes and References

Sometime looking backward
into this future, straining
neck and eyes I'll meet your shadow
with its enormous eyes
you who will want to know
what this was all about.
                    —Adrienne Rich, *Midnight Salvage*

A WORLD LESS PERFECT FOR DYING IN

WHAT I LOOK FOR IN A POEM

Clear blue light
       A single voice, cold, in need of fire
              Any world less perfect for dying in

Full circles
       The black of night waiting at my bedside
              Everything I have ever buried

I. EVERYTHING I HAVE EVER BURIED

We were the uncountable stars, at first.
We were nothing at first, and the light
of what was already over still in it.
                              —Larry Levis, *Elegy*

WHAT WE'VE COME TO EXPECT FROM BEAUTY

I.

It is midnight. My apartment is quiet.
I can hear the cars rushing down Somerville Avenue,
my neighbor shedding her clothes to the floor—
the faint shuffle of feet, the scrape of a hanger.
And I think about her now.

Just one hour ago, stopped at the corner,
a woman knocked on my window before I could turn.
I leaned over and spoke with her in the narrow space
between the door frame and top of the glass.

She asked if she could sit in my car,
if I wanted to talk a little, the black of night
shining deep in the gaps between her teeth,
her face a little gray and tired.

Sometimes I think that is all
this world has to offer—hapless invitations,
the quiet offertory my neighbor makes
each night as she undresses.

She knows I can hear. She asked and I told her.
I said it without a smile because I believed it did not matter,
though tonight I need to imagine her in that moment
before she slips into a long tee shirt and nothing more,

her skin shining in the dark,
a star and her own source of light
traveling through miles and miles of darkness.

II.

Let us suppose you haven't yet felt included,
that my insisting we have pined together is
nothing more than that—my pining and you haven't
wished beauty to find you, to welcome you to its table
where you would sit, leaning over your elbows,

slipping slowly forward till your hands touch
like moon light descended on soft, forgiving snow.

But I believe that we all, at the very least,
should have some. Beauty, that is.
Maybe even just a little more. That

even in a poem about beauty
we must be moved to see its two sure hands
and how our own fit perfectly inside them.

CONFIDING IN THE PRISON GUARD

"After me comes one more powerful than I . . . I baptize you with water, but he will baptize you with the Holy Spirit."   —Mark 1:7-8

You see these garments? I made them.
With these hands. See here? This is the very place
I cut myself on the blade of my knife.
See how it has healed, how the flesh
has closed itself again, grown together, pink and new?
And this belt. I tanned it from the same beast.
She brought me to within sight of these city walls.
Then collapsed. I held her head in my lap,
stroking her neck until the sun set low,
and the night was filled with fire. It is true
what they say about the death of the day.
My soul, too, will rise above the parting sun soon enough.
No doubt you will be the one to set it free.

Ah, these hands. They have touched his head. His hair
filled my palms, slipped over and through my fingers,
until my hands were hidden, as if they, too, grew peaceably from
his skin. He said nothing when I lowered him into the river, his
body weightless. I was afraid I'd lose him to the current, his body
swept downstream. What would come of me then? I swear, when
he stood, the water swimming down his face and plunking into the
river around him like fingers on a harp, the day gave way to night,
the sun smeared across the edge of the earth, then raced across the
sky in rivers of light.

I understand I am to lose my head. Will you grant me this then,
that I might wash my face and hair? And would you also share
what I have told you? Not now. But after Herodias has slipped
her fingers through my mane and lifted my bodiless head above her
own, into the light, my blood dripping to the floor, the shadow of
night drifting calmly over everything.

SHOOSTER

One summer, the neighbors directly behind
my grandparents' house brought home a rooster.
My two brothers and I named him Shooster.
We spent the whole season strutting and clucking

back and forth along the chain-link fence that
divided the lots into yards. In return, Shooster
would strum the fence with his sharp beak
and bark us back to the middle of the lawn.

One day, after lunch, Shooster did not come
no matter which tone we called in or how hard
we rattled the fence, the seed we scattered
just before going in still spotting the dry Tennessee soil.

Later that night, dining with the neighbors, we found him.
Only we felt we knew him too well, and after the table
was cleared, we slipped the bones into a plastic bag
and took them out into the dark.

Kneeling beside the fence in the faint glow of the porch light
that barely reached this part of the yard, we three dug into
the ground with my grandfather's trowel to a depth
we felt would keep our friend safe from more harm.

We patted the earth down with our feet and sprinkled loose dirt
over the tiny mound. Not to hide what we had done. But because
we felt revealed, this the first lesson in who we would make
ourselves available for: so much becoming us from so little.

We bowed our heads, each offering his own prayer.
Then, we just walked away. Each to his own room.
Near. But not too near.
Satellites. Waiting for sleep.

WATCHING THE SANDHILL MIGRATION, FIRST LIGHT EASTER MORNING, IN NEBRASKA'S PLATTE RIVER VALLEY

Together   in a fluttering cloud   against muted winds tripping
over bright red-crested heads   over this narrow stretch of river
where the earth is still young   still littered with still-water basins
where spiders build their webs   under every broken grass
where no lights shine   even under brightest moon
they lift
           follow the nod   of a single beak or unfolded
wing   long legs trailing behind   calling out loud as jet engines
reflecting off the water below still ringed with waves   whose
every center's filled   with *my very first glimpse of heaven*   even
though I'm sure it isn't true   but something must be said
before this moment passes   which is   at every moment's
center   of our lives   for now.

JESUS WAS A HANDSOME MAN

It's clear to see   lochs of pure light   eyes and the oceans in
them   perfect for wading in

Elvis was a handsome man   too   swimming with fire
a voice too free to keep as his own   roaming alone without him
now

My father knew him   Memphis Tennessee   where no one feels
at home alone beside the river   that treacherous ride into the gulf

And when he sang   we were perfect sanctuaries   desire's desire
seeded there

Elvis knew Jesus   raised his voice   into perfect clouds
with perfect rain   over our heads   to reach him

Somewhere between   the heavens and the fields
we are sure to die   (and yes   I mean my father too)

an Elvis refrain   astride the carriage of our tongues
the earth holding us close   with inelegant treason

ELEGY TO THE HEART AND ALL THAT IT ENDURES

I.
Yesterday, a young man was hit by a car,
here, at this very spot, in front of this café.

He stepped off the curb out into the street
and kept on walking without looking.

The driver never had a chance.
And later he would say that

to the boy, in his hospital bed,
unconscious but breathing.

I did not know the young man,
but he was the same age I was

the first time I said I Love You and knew
what it meant, felt it with my whole body

as if I had been lifted from the ground by something
so much larger than me I could not have stopped it.

II.
Maybe it is unfair to compare myself
to the young man who was run down.

Surely he would tell me the two things
are not the same and he would show me

the scars and the bruises that remain.
Can love do this, he might ask,

fingering the raised white tissue that
streaks across the leg where he was hit,

where the bone broke through the skin
like a hand reaching out to the heavens.

ELEGY TO YOUNG BOYS JUMPING OFF THE END OF THE DOCK

One boy,
taller than the rest, his head rising above

them all, takes his place in line, pushing
and shoving. He inches his way slowly forward

until the only thing between him and water is open air.
There, he turns away after standing too long before jumping,

slips past the others, who watch in silence as they
step aside to let him pass. Not one joke is made.

And when it seems that every last boy will follow his lead,
thinking now of shallower water, they quickly

turn away, laughter spilling from their mouths,
again pounding through the water's surface.

There is so much strength needed to be a boy
of this age, each knowing his fate is manhood

and that he must take to practicing now.
This is nothing a boy can change.

No doubt this boy will return tomorrow and make the jump.
He will get there first and stay one jump longer,

fly into the blue green lake with so much air
beneath him, the other boys already heading

back to the dorms, lake water drying off their skin
in the breeze made by brisk walking.

WHAT YOU SHOULD KNOW ABOUT MY MOTHER

I.

A minister's daughter.
A good wife.
A good mother.

Ask her what it means to be one.
A good mother that is.
And she will tell you.

It is a little like sunlight—
dying slowly,
every day.

It is giving up—
because you must always,
always, give.

The list is long.
And you will listen.
Because you will trust her.

Her every word too, too much
like everything you have ever had
to leave behind, to ever let these go.

II.

Every summer, for as long as I can remember, my mother
trimmed the eight foot hedge that surrounded the back yard.

She unraveled the orange extension cord,
plugged one end into the house, the other into the trimmer,

then climbed up and down the ladder for half the summer
until she had whittled away all the excess growth.

When she was done, her sweat drying into small
white rivers of salt, she would stand in the middle of the lawn,

lean on the trimmer that refused to bend beneath her,
to admire the clean and squared edges against

the summer sky as if to dare a single rogue branch
to stray, wave alone in the breeze, so she could

tuck it back among the others, shaping the world
into a safe, manageable place one would even call pretty.

III.

The man my mother loves is dying.
He knows it. She knows it. But,
that is the way they like things.
No surprises and every day as much
the same as the day they first met:
the two of them new and beautiful
and the entire world around them
perfect for living and dying in.

IV.

It was important to my mother
that her children learn how to swim.

She took us all, one by one, down to the park
for lessons and watched from the observation deck

high above the pool as we each learned
to carve the water with our hands, our heads

bobbing in and out for fresh breaths of air,
all done with simple, mechanical precision.

She herself never learned though she returned
time and time again to the water. Each time

she sank, unable to pull the water to her
stroke after stroke to ever make it hers.

Yet, she could lie on her back
for hours, float like a lily,

stare up into the sky, spin back
and forth in the gentle waves made

by passing swimmers. "It's like having
to hold all of that water, and I just can't,"

she once told me, driving home, hair
still wet, drips plunking down on hot vinyl.

She eyed the road ahead, gaze fixed
just above the single wave, buoyed between steadied palms

steering us toward a braver world,
cradling all but the will's permission.

V.

Ever since her last birthday, my mother has been
giving her things away. Her house
narrowed down to what she needs most.
This summer, she gave me her garden trowels.

My mother tended her gardens in the morning.
I followed her sometimes, out into the lawn, kicked
the grass with bare feet, brushed clean dark stripes
into the shaggy, dewy carpet.

She brought her wicker basket to the edge
and left it there. Trowel in hand,
she dove barefooted into the bay of green leaves
that parted briefly then cuddled up against her ankles.

She would wander up and down the rows
hands punched to her hips,
bending only to retrieve the mature fruit
or to cut away the choking growths.

And each pass yielded goods.
Proof of every hour's labor,
arranged by length and hue,
punctuated each conquered aisle.

When the harvesting was done, the morning
giving way beneath the sun, she would wipe
loose soil from tender skins and fill her basket,
sturdiest bodies first until they eclipsed the brim.

Even then the handles bent beneath the weight
of everything she left clinging to the vines, of desire
still aspiring to promise, of the impractical longing
of longing for death's hedging will inspire.

THE FIRST OF THE LAST DAYS OF TREE CLIMBING

For most of my youth, my father was a tree.
And climbing was a small retreat, my back to everything,
leaves holding fast against the breeze.

What did other matters matter—the spines of books uncreased
hedge trimmings and clippings scattered across the lawn—
when well-shaded roots knuckled up from cool grasses,

or when unbending limbs carried me up, fit firmly
beneath each step toward flickering blue and sun,
the ways of childhood still too much with me.

I was happy this way. Swinging sometimes. Palms
callused by bark. Until I fell. Landed flat on my back. Wind
pushed from my lungs so entirely I thought I was dying.

When my breath came back, those slow promising gulps,
I gathered myself from the ground and ran home.
Nearly fell over my father watching from the patio door.

Looking up only then to see how tall he stood above me,
I dropped in a heap on the last step up. Ashamed
for coming so close to death.

My father helped me into the house. And though
he never said a word, I knew he knew. I knew also that my fall
meant nothing when he led me to his reading chair

where I fell asleep, leaning against the arm, my head
on his shoulder, his breath rustling my unkempt hair
still hot from so much sun.

PROVING GROUNDS

We cut through the park again, head home from the public pool,
so my brother and I—mother's urging shrugged aside—can look

for bottles in the tall grasses that surround the horseshoe pits. And
we have become good collectors. Toss new-found labels into shirts

fashioned smartly into satchels, pennies closer to some prize
we've yet to name, the pantry shelves, now *nearly three rows deep*,

our mother's concern growing, the summer
already too long by late June.

This morning the pits are filled—green and brown bottles
gleam with dew—and without a word between us,

we smash glittering glass against stead-fast stakes instead,
look up only after every bottle is gone,

early morning sun sharp on each severed edge,
the smell of beer lingering on our fingers.

When we return home, our shirts on our backs, mother asks
why we have no bottles for her to rinse and sort,

washtub braced against her hip. I tell her about
the bottles, about the chiming, about the way they glittered,

colored the sands, as she stares us down, the collection,
my brother and me, fingers strumming empty tub.

Without a word, she grabs two rakes from the garage,
drives us to the pits, stands over us, arms crossed,

until sand and glass are raked into small,
even mounds. As soon as we are done, we dump

the evidence of our work into the nearby bin,
follow our mother to the car, to the task we know

must lie ahead. The burn of hard labor still in our backs
and arms, we believe even then that what we did was not wrong,

maybe even beautiful, the weight of mother's will
giving way beneath midmorning sun.

BECAUSE WE WERE ASSIGNED TO WRITE BAD FICTION

We were trying to write something bad. To explore what makes bad fiction. The woman with hair like olive branches wrote to her grandfather. A kindly man. Who whittled wood on his front porch. The letter she wrote was filled with the voice of the young girl she knew he imagined when he thought of her. She read the fiction to us as if she had to articulate that this was clearly not the woman she was. That clearly the tone in her voice carried the weight of each unspoken word. And, when she looked up from her small notebook, the room was silent for just a little while longer. We each envisioned him opening that very letter, his whittling set aside, the knife blade sledding through the glued lip of the envelope flap, the starling he had been carving, waiting patiently in his lap. In that silence, the pain of her love rose into the air. What the letter didn't say was this: that the olive tree loved a woman. That she never planned to marry. That he would never raise her children into the very lap his starling rested in as he read. And then each of us imagined the letter we would write, our own omission branding our love no matter where or whom we loved, no matter how well or how poorly we loved, the earth rotating us away from that very moment, dislodging us from the story that would surely save our lives, if we felt the slightest pull from it at all.

THE DEAF COUPLE, THEIR FIGHT,
AND THE HEALING HANDS OF ANGELS

She cuts the air into shreds. Her fingers
work sharply like scissors blades. His fists,
oil rigs, pound the table top, pump up and down
between jingling plates and silverware.

A sharp slice of his hand over the table's edge
catches a bus boy on the arm, relieves him
of his dishes, which clatter to the floor.
Glasses and plates scatter into smaller and smaller pieces.

The man stands and begins
to help pick up the mess,
tries hard to say he's sorry,
to speak and gather at the same time.

The bus boy catches the man's wrists,
shakes his head to say no.
A bridge for a moment over the wreckage,
they look into each other's eyes.

With a simple nod, a jab really, it is done.
They stand, and the bus boy lets go,
their hands dropping to their sides,
relieved of the rising heat of words.

TOMORROW, AND TOMORROW, AND TOMORROW

We are sometimes dreams
when we are here
lying low among the daisies,
the husks of grass
and oranges.

We were better intentioned
before we landed, though;
a heap of ended everything,
waiting to rise less complicated
for the wide open space we relaxed into.

True, there may be bluer skies,
but not here, not now.
And green has rarely been greener,
or more, just like these fields
seen from afar.

Dare to take our willful leisure
out of the frame—
blue and green are all that is left
except for the slow, slow
accumulation of time.

Yesterdays *have* lighted fools
the way to dusty death.
This moment's rest
is a makeshift armor
against both sound and fury.

From the slim
rake of hills
that frost the horizon
we are less than
the shadow of a cloud.

But, let us prefer it
this way, for now,
our backs pressing down firmly,
the light giving way
beneath the weight.

A NEARLY TRUE POEM ABOUT POSTCARDS FROM THE MOMA SHE NEVER KNEW SHE WANTED BEFORE TODAY

one was a photo of a photo
of itself.

on the back, it read:
wish you were here.

       one was a painted brick,
       worth its weight in postage.

one was a flock of birds,
that spelled out her name when it flew overhead.

       one was a series of books,
       each with a single highlighted word
       she had to find to glean its meaning.

one was a flowerbed. just because.

       together, they applied for a NEA,
       to support their correspondence.

       then wrote grant letters to each other
       that explained the need for art in their exchange.

       eventually the stacks of letters became the art the NEA
       supported.

MOMA set her postcards on fire.
the smoke rose into the clouds, which made it rain.

and when it reached her,
she could feel the words in the drops on her skin.

they plucked at her like a harp.

once MOMA sent an EKG.
the caption read, "this here, this peak right here, is the
exact moment when I thought of you."

MOMA sometimes whispers her name into paper.
so when she holds it to a candle, she believes the shadow

like knowing of heart beats
before the heart.

IF THE WEATHER HOLDS, SHE SAID

Though she could just as easily have meant
the bridge they have been building,

tie and rail inching through the blue,
framing elusive air.

From bridge's end,
trees, slow rising skies,

the pond, the silver backs of geese
resting on the banks,

the blankets of bread crumbs
all disappear into endless birds drifting through

weathered ties here and there like
immutable memories, calling.

Sometimes,
at the peak of working,

those heavy sounds of hammers,
the whistling of drills

drift over the horizon
like the very tracks beneath their feet.

Surely, they will check
to see if it is true,

lift each foot carefully,
eye the soles of their shoes,

test the rails where they stand,
where a sudden future's forming,

in every piercing
spoke of sun.

SO MUCH GOOD WEATHER

I sit down beside you   at the kitchen counter   with two mugs
filled with good warm coffee   Gus is between our stools
each of us   reaching to pet his head   scratch under his chin
talking about   how everyone needs this   a good dog
nodding   as we say it.

The back door is open   Though it is a little too cool   it is
unseasonably warm   for New England in November
So we keep the door open   our breath misting   just a little
the days   as nice as this one   coming to an end   even now
while the two of us   are talking   and petting   saying
everyone   when we really mean   ourselves   when what
we want to say   is love   how everyone needs love
how it fills the space   we are dreaming in   and still
fits here   between us   within these narrow kitchen walls
like so much good weather.

FREE THIS POEM. IT WANTS TO FLY

You told me once about the day
your professor asked your class to write
a poem about milkweed then loosed
a pod full into the air, the window open,
the sun shining in, a new autumn breeze blowing.

Everyone in the room watched closely,
heads turned as white tufts passed by—
ghosts, like the spirits of loved ones
freed into the open air.

One seed floated down into your hair.
Your professor walked by and lifted it out, held it up for you to
see. You each smiled. But not at each other.
To yourselves, thinking hard
about who you wanted most to be set free.

FOR A BRIEF TIME I WALKED AMONGST THEM

Jesus appeared to his disciples, by the Sea of Tiberias. It happened his way.
—John 21:1

If only you could have seen their faces when
the nets they cast filled entirely with fish,
their arms too tired to pull the nets in.
The look stayed with each one of them until
they died and like the sun hitting water even then.

WHAT WE RETURN TO

I.

I have only once been close enough to the ocean
to touch it. The waves broke against the narrow ledge
where I sat with the woman I thought I knew.

While we watched the ocean reach and reach for shore
she explained that in an hour, this ledge, too,
would be consumed by water.

At the airport that night, she hugged me,
whispered good-bye in my ear. I knew what she meant.
I slept the entire flight until the moment we touched down.

My body was still weighted heavily with sleep
as I made my way down the empty aisle
past the flight attendant who smiled, welcomed me home.

Snow sweeping across my back and shoulders,
I headed down the stairs into the light so blue
I could have sworn I was drowning.

II.

The next morning when I woke, I found the earth
covered in a fresh blanket of snow. It was as if
the clouds had grown tired of holding it and had laid it down to
take a rest.
In the distance, I could hear the sound of others shoveling—
the scrape of metal on cement followed by the near silent tossing
aside of wet snow, which made a faint, faint thudding,
like the slow steady beat of a heart finally at rest.

III.

Last night on the street
I saw a friend I had not seen in years.

She told me she had been living in France
and had only just returned.

We talked in the cold for what
seemed like hours.

I was amazed when she spoke.
Everything she said sounded new.

Even my name, which she said again and again,
as if each time she said it

what she meant to say was home,
I am home, I am home.

IV.

Two tall pines stand in the front of the building where I live.
They are old and their branches are strong.

I know because yesterday I climbed one, lifting myself
hand over hand up into these strong arms, close to the

trunk where no needles grew. I nearly climbed to the top,
the branches finally too weak to hold me

began to bend under my weight. I could see over
the houses on my street and for many streets beyond.

I sat down on the branch where I was standing.
And stayed. An hour. Maybe more.

The sun took its time creeping over the horizon.
The entire sky turned from blue to pink to red and back to blue.

It looked so close I reached out to touch it.
I might still be there now

if my fingers and face had not begun to grow numb,
the wind weaving through my hair,

my head leaning back against the trunk standing
its ground, a reminder of all I have never left behind.

II. A WORLD LESS PERFECT FOR DYING IN

The thing I came for:
the wreck itself and not the story of the wreck
the thing itself and not the myth.
—Adrienne Rich, *Diving Into the Wreck*

A COMPREHENSIVE LIST OF WHAT THE EARTH
OWES ME FOR MY TIME HERE SO FAR

Warmth.
A fire that reaches
the heart first, consuming the flesh
from the inside.

Liberty.
Not freedom, but liberty.
So that I may call my voice
home.

Fearlessness.
Or, at the very least,
a heart larger than my fist
that my heart may always win.

Love.
Yes, love, too.
But because it
needed me.

A place to die in.
One with clean corners.
One with even walls: one perfect
for perfect slumber.

Everything I once believed in, living on without me.
Like trees that have lived through winter after winter after winter
without their leaves, without their beautiful,
beautiful leaves.

PLANNING OUR DEPARTURE

Leaving nothing to chance, we start the day
by sharing our only surviving dreams.

Mine is simple. The two of us driving nowhere
with little regard for the drive.

In yours, we are rowing. Taking our time.
Taking turns at the oars.

We make nothing more of them than that,
that we have shared them.

You roll away from me, hand dropping
against the box spring,

as if to usher this bed into motion, into
one last feat of greatness though nothing on it stirs.

While we lie here, storm clouds
settle in above us,

rain gathers in their sagging bellies, felled cotton seed
invades every grassless patch of ground below.

I half expect to find this bed covered too,
mistake loose down against my pillow

for some ambitious seed that made it through
the screen beside this bed, seeking some higher,

safer place to land, who knows what falling is,
how it ends where no light reaches and never has.

Not even in the highest noonday sun when
the shadows are but charcoal blemishes no bigger than a sigh.

So much goes unsaid between us now.
The day passes us by slowly, drifts over

the trenches where we lie, the hours ahead
still unfulfilled except by all we cannot manage

the strength to save, by the rain, cold and hard,
falling from the sky to the earth where we wait.

We insist on waging our losses against an hour more
of sleep, against facing our certain departure from this room,

or from any room just like this where we may have landed,
seeking shelter from all we can't possibly begin to begin.

WHY I HAVE NOT WRITTEN BACK BEFORE NOW, AT THE WELCOME APPROACH OF SPRING

I.
All of this snow.

It is still above the knee
in the middle of the yard
and so cold it warms.

When I stood in it,
hurdled over the shoveled embankment
from the path to the door
into the yielding flesh,

my heart gave in as easily.

II.
The houses across the street
are turning their backs
on spring's first sun.
What else can be done
after so many
winter full days?

III.
No two snowflakes are alike.
Not even any of these
falling now.

Perhaps too much is made of this.
As if we really suspect that they are,
or at least two of them are,
and we should always
be looking.

IV.
The puddle at the end of my block
covers the entire intersection.

It is more water than Yuma will see
during the driest parts of June.
I have measured.

Later, when the sun climbs down
from its seat in the sky, the puddle
will freeze over completely.

Solid ice that will
support every car or truck
that crawls across its back.

And nothing will change this
except the warm hand of the sun.

We call this inflexibility love,
this undying reliance
on the touch of one hand.

V.

Nearly six feet of snow
has fallen since November.
Imagine if it had been
anything else
but snow.
Anything at all.

VI.

My mother knitted her way through long winters.
The afghan at the foot of my bed is the careful work
of one December.
Red, yellow, orange, all surrounded
by black, by the nothingness of cold.

I used to curl up beneath it,
let the dark edges touch the ground around me,
covered only in the warm colors of spring.
It was the only way I could warm the center of my heart.

When I moved away to where the winters stretch across the land

for so many uninterrupted days, she insisted that I have it,
hung it over my shoulders, fastened like a shawl, my heart
too full with all I cannot have to keep from growing cold.

PREMONITION OF AN EARLY RETIREMENT

It comes while the syrup thickens,
the heat of the fire inching into the pan from below.

I stir slowly,
to ensure it will not burn around the edges,

resisting the urge to dip a finger,
to test its readiness, its sweetest, purest dilution,

so that everything will taste the way I was promised
as I paid for my bottle of "pure heaven" across that small table.

Tiny bottles, just like mine, glistened in the sun.
And they were all honeyed and thick like his voice,

the man whose work is now mine, whose skin was ridged and
rough as tree bark. At least, that is how I imagine it to be

because how else would he know, because how else will I know,
if all this waiting is not in vain.

ON LOOKING AT A PHOTO OF TWO SOLDIERS ON THE WALL IN COSTELLO'S BAR, SAINT PAUL

Both men are smiling. One man is leaning on the jeep's bumper,
rifle rooted to the ground, hand holding ever so loosely.

The other man stands beside him, holding before him the rising
sun against snow-white cloth.

And you are staring at them, too, head turned over your shoulder,
describing to me what cannot be seen:

the man they must have killed for his flag
still lying just out of view of the road where they found him
sleeping,

as if he had forgotten about the war or simply ceased to care,
the sun overhead against a cloudless sky the last thing he saw
before drifting off.

Your back still turned to me, you tell me of the time you were
fishing and were dragged under by the current and carried down-
stream.

You came to a stop near the bank where the river
had faded to a shallow brook and could not carry you further,

and you slept because you were far from home and tired.
It is hard now to imagine the story of the photo

could be told any other way, the two of us with nothing more to
say, staring at the wall, the two men holding up the flag to us

as if we, too, were lying back into the tall grass as midday,
leaving so much left undone, the wind touching everything.

JUST OFF THE HENNEPIN BRIDGE

From here, downtown is magnificent. Bold. Stark.
Bright, against the dull haze of cloud cover. Light
fits so easily into so many different places:

in the office windows across the river, in the face of the moon,
in the puddles that still dot the earth after this afternoon's rain.
Even in these bricks in the street, as if placed here like seeds.

To think, last night, just a few blocks from here two men
were shot to death over nothing. The man who did it was
found at home, sitting in front of the TV. He was watching

the news for his story. The men were no one he knew.
Said he kissed each man, full on the lips before he shot
them. Told them Jesus loved them and they would be

saved. He just needed their wallets. He needed to eat
and he wanted a beer. Nothing more. Nothing personal.
Man's gotta eat, ya know. Man's gotta eat.

Trick or treaters approach me, howling and laughing.
When they pass me, they pass by silently. Single file.
Eyes straight ahead. Fingers clutching their candy bags.

I watch them disappear around the bend. A squad car drifts up
slowly. The man at the wheel tells me that I should move on.
Maybe because I'm smiling, because I seem too interested, and I'm
writing all this down.

NIGHTHAWKS

(on looking at Edward Hopper's painting, Nighthawks)

Nightfall is in for the evening,
resting on everything with its heavy shadows,
tired from lifting every heavy wave
upon its back.

And leaning into tall buildings
has never once been easy.
For now, its long arms hug the counter beneath our feet,
and drape across our shoulders.

We each bow a little beneath the weight,
are that much closer to our cups because of it,
that much closer to the ground beneath us.
We will meet up again then. There.

For now, we sit and drink,
lean back a little sometimes
to uncrease the curl in our spines
or lean our faces in to the glow of electric light,

the way we might to break the water's surface one last time
before slipping down, far beneath the waves,
the shadow of night beneath our heels
even then.

TOWARD SOME PROVINCIAL HEAVEN

on looking at a photo from the exhibit, Lake Street USA *by Wing Young Huie*

Three girls sit at the feet of their father,
who is blocking the sun from the backs of their necks.

Their knees are bent, jutting out before them,
toes just breaching the edge of the street, their heels in the gutter.

One girl is rubbing her eyes. She is holding her doll
in the crook of her elbow, neck pinched, button eyes bulging and
afraid.

The middle girl leans away, back against the legs of her father,
eyes focused on the face behind the camera.

I've seen that look in her eyes before, on a cat I carried,
dying, from the street. It skidded off the bumper of the car that
never slowed,

that kept on going, the cat's legs twisting and clawing at the air,
reaching for ground, as if falling from a tree.

The third girl has her eyes closed, hands folded in her lap, head
craned just a little, chin pointing into the air, street lights reflecting
off the glass behind her head.

Her lips are parted. All their lips are parted, each stopped in the
middle of a word. What each of them is saying, I feel I am
supposed to know.

A NIGHT LIKE THIS

Turning onto my street, I brake hard to avoid a man who crosses
right in front of me. I roll down my window to apologize.
But before I can, he leans down, tells me he needs four dollars
because his car has been repaired and he is that much short. The
air is cold and his breath, heavy with alcohol, slumbers into a heavy
mist as soon as it leaves his lips. He has no hat or gloves. Just a
lightweight jacket that is too small, his shoulders pushing through
the seams. He is tired and has been walking a great distance. I can
see it in his long stares that have no destination. Between sighs, he
has managed to slip two daughters into his tale. They are cold,
hungry, eager to see their mother who is waiting for them at home.
I want to give him money. But I have heard this story before.
From a man who approached me on my way home, groceries in
each hand, on a night like this. He followed me for two blocks,
asking and asking, before I turned to face him, told him to go away,
to leave me alone, the anger in my voice striking like a fist. He
stopped and faded away. Just disappeared. When I got home, I
slammed the door so hard behind me my shoulder ached and there
was nothing left to do but sleep, to wake in the morning as if this
all had been a dream. Which is why, tonight, all I can manage to
say is sorry, I am truly sorry, as he disappears around the nearest
storefront, the last traces of sunlight slipping into his footprints
already filling with snow.

GOD IS DEAD, AND HOW WE KNOW

The woman across the hall was the first to suspect it was true.
Usually, the sweet or savory scent of any baked goods
would call Him to His door.

A moment standing there, oven mitts between hot glass and her
palms was all it ever took. No knocking. And when the door
would open, that familiar silence between them would spill out into
the hall, rap lightly on each and every door, though no one heard.

So when it happened, this passing away this way alone behind
closed door, only the cats that roamed the halls at night knew and
gathered to pace back and forth, pawing the thin slice of light just
above the floor.

Yes, I'm sure of it, she said, receiver held firmly to her ear
afraid the meaning might escape her words
through the narrowest passage of doubt, hers or theirs.

When the firefighters arrived, the noise of their plying wood
with axe blades drew a small crowd to their doorways at last.
Once inside, standing by the body was hard.

One of the men toed Him. The others looked up, searching
for the hole through which He might have fallen, though not a one
would mention this if ever asked of what he saw.

When at last they looked down again, she held out the cake,
still warm in her mitted hands. With a single nod, she urged they
eat. So they did, licking their fingers eagerly, until it was gone.

The pan finally empty, she squeezed their arms, grateful.
Each one of them, the woman too, though she only ate but
crumbs, felt full, sucking the cake off their teeth behind their lips,
until they felt nothing there.

UNDER THE MISSING AND INNUMERABLE STARS

Sitting in your car, parked directly behind my own,
our two cars the only ones on the street now
the hour of midnight having passed us long ago, you
tell me of your failed marriage and release your terrible sadness.
It started with nights alone on the couch, before the fireplace.
Sometimes with wine. Sometimes without. You giving
yourself slowly to the idea that you deserved more somehow.
And this idea grew until you left him. You took nothing
with you except the great immeasurable hole that only love
lost can make. In the dark, in that quiet small space, I reached
my hand out and touched your leg, rested my palm over
your thigh. You did not move it, but reached your own hand down
and held mine, both of us resting there at what could have been
either the beginning or the end of the world, our eyes fixed ahead
on hundreds of stars whose light we would only see once
and then never again.

ENDURANCE

Talking over coffee   the conversation shifts from baseball
to old age   and his grandfather is dying of Alzheimer's
I say the only thing   I think can make it better   that I lost
my grandmother this way   and I tell him also   that it will
get worse

Two full days   after we arrived in Memphis   we were sitting
around the TV   my mother   my father   my sister and I
when she turned   to my grandfather   and asked   *when
will Vivy   and the kids arrive*   My mother rose from her seat
kneeled before her mother   cradled her hands like robin eggs
looked her in the eye   told her   *we are here
we are all here*

It's hard to imagine   how much worse a thing like this could be
but it whittled her away   year after year   into nothing   I
tell him this also   About the nothing   To prepare him for
what I know he must endure   To show him I managed

And before long   we have moved on to talking about baseball
again   taking that necessary leap   putting the rest
of the world aside   just long enough   to forgive each other
of our deepest sadness.

MOTHERS AND SONS

Across the table, you hold up the paper
to show me a picture. And, as if the distance

between us were too great for me to navigate,
you recite the story headline, your face hidden

behind the thin shield of words: "George
Mallory's Last Moments Atop Mount Everest."

The picture is of his body, still lying where
it came to rest after his fatal fall, the summit

of Everest climbing high above him in the distance.
His body is perfectly preserved, clothes shredded

into coils, exposed flesh frozen solid and glistening
in the light of the sun. He clings to the face of the mountain,

as if carved from the very rock his fingers still claw,
his body is still fit, the muscles of his back still tense and strained.

You fold the paper around to the final page,
the photo now buried, the pages crackle like ice.

The light of the morning sun drifts over your face,
exposes the lines that have driven themselves into

your skin slowly, without my detection. You are
not so young as I remember you even yesterday.

I want to reach over to you and with my thumb,
wipe away the lines, to see that same woman

my father would fall in love with some day when the two of you
were young so that I might know how to lose you, also.

I still hold on to a story you once told me,
knowingly, of a woman who died while climbing.

She froze to death, beyond the reach of the sun's warmth,
cradled in snow so white it glowed. Her husband climbed

after her to bury her, to know the flesh that had
carried him to love without pause one last time.

Soon the morning sun will rise to its peak. It will
warm the earth. All of it. Even its poles and crests.

You and I will cast our shadows out behind us
with adolescent recklessness—pure faith. They will

return again at day's end. The lines time has forged
into your skin left stranded by the descending sun.

TO HAVE AND TO HOLD

For that brief moment, I watch
as you fit your hands around mother's throat,
press your thumbs against her trachea,
your face calm, as if squeezing a melon.

I stand and speak your name. *Charles.*
You pause, thinking the voice has somehow
passed up through your grip. You release
her neck, hold your hands up to the light.

And then it comes again. My small voice. *Charles?*
Nothing more is said. You turn to me,
hands still raised, two shallow and empty bowls
you have never been able to fill before now.

Calmly, mother turns her back and walks away.
You walk back to the sink, submerge your hands
into the soap and pull the stopper to let the water drain,
revealing the dishes cleaned and ready to dry.

You lift all of them, one at a time, drying rack filling slowly
until you are done. You wipe off your hands,
wadding the towel into a ball, a small new planet
to toss aside. And it is over. Everything is over.

MY FATHER'S SON, MY BROTHER

I clutch the pavement with the tips of my toes,
empty pedals still spinning, brake lights glaring
angrily in my face. The car is filled entirely with your things
and sits low over the rear tire wells.

That is how I know you are leaving. That,
and I heard you say it, pulling free from father's hands,
stepping away from the wall where he pinned and dissected you,
named you unfit and unworthy.

You rise from the car. Hands circle
above me like birds of prey until they grab
and lift me into the air, my face even with yours.
You will never . . . ever . . . do that again, you say,

shaking me, fingers clutching my arms
and pressing them into my sides.
My tears seem to be the only things that end this.
You set me down in the grass alongside my toppled tricycle,

say nothing, quickly disappear into the sea
of your belongings, ready now to drive away.
There is nothing more I can do to stop you.
I wave. My palm, empty, faces out into your world.

Up ahead the road shimmers. I know
it is just the heat rising. But I imagine it is water
and you have to go, your hands cemented with sorrow,
the weight of the world already pulling you under.

CAMERA SHY
                    —for my father

Slowly, you rise from your armchair and slide
to the seat next to me on the couch, our knees

touching. I let you ease the yearbook from my
hands, surprised by your eagerness to hunt out

the face of The King. Until now, I never knew
you to care. To you, he was a punk, a

delinquent, unworthy of your time.
The details you recall help us to narrow the search:

which hour English class; who his friends were;
who your friends were, why your paths never crossed.

We pause over the photo of the yearbook staff
long enough to find you standing in the last row,

smiling wide, your arms draped warmly over the shoulders
of your friends beside you. A photo you were certain

you had missed *because you never showed your face
on picture day.* On the very next page, we find

you again, posing with the speech team, again
standing in the back, again smiling wide. *Because*

I was always tall you say with pride as if this mattered
more to you than did being a part of the team.

It is no great surprise when, a few pages later,
we also find you as president of the drama club.

It does not surprise me, yet it is strange to see.
I have searched countless times through our family albums,

56

and have never found a picture with your arms around me
or your lips pressed against my cheek in a fatherly kiss.

I often wonder if you can still picture the day you left—I held
the door as you stormed out of the house, shoulders shrugged,

hands raised in defeat and bare as winter trees as if we
had robbed you of your leaves. Maybe this is what you

mean when you say that you are camera shy, that you wish
to remain unknown, unrecognized for the things you have done.

At last the search has come to an end. I am the one who
finds him in the Glee Club photo. We have searched

the entire book. This is the only place we find him. The King,
Elvis Presley, like you, is standing in the back row, smiling

a big southern smile, half a head taller than the others. You
can't believe we have found him at all, that we have found

him on a page opposite you, both your heads just above
the crowd, your bodies hidden and completely out of view.

SILENT MARCH

I am surprised to hear him say that he
no longer plays, my brother's piano now a mantel
for picture frames and vases, and I slip away
to find the first recording of him we made.

When I find the tape, I pull it from its forgotten place
and hold it up for everyone to see.
It is the tape of our family at Christmas
thirty years before.

Our father interviewed us all one at a time.
My brother played the piano rather than speak—
original jazz riffs and a little bit of blues.
It is why I began the search at all,
to prove to everyone what he could do then,
so young and without lessons.

But nothing can be heard.
The tape, too old and muffled,
murmurs softly like someone trapped in sleep.

Mother flips her dishtowel over her shoulder
then heads back to the kitchen.
His wife pats him on the knee and smiles.
Our sister shrugs then picks up her book to read,
the two of us left listening to all we have lost—
the tape, our voices, this snapshot of our lives.

He rises from his seat, slowly, deliberately,
into this silent march from our past,
relieved nothing can be heard,
that there is nothing he must defend,
the reels still spinning, the sounds drifting
in and out, and in and out,
like whispers in another room
we must pretend we do not hear.

PHOTO TAKEN OF ME ATOP THE WORLD TRADE CENTER, NOVEMBER 1995

At the last second   I stuck my arm   out over the railing
pinched the distant statue   between my finger and thumb
smiling into the wind   the sun fading behind me   into steel-
blue harbor.

And all for a laugh   never expecting to find this   buried in a
box that you gave to me   filled with my things   a note
wrapped around it I had written for you:

>   ...whose likeness was
>   in posture only, in "the way they
>   held out their hand."

A line from my own poem about love   because they all are
even this one though I meant for it to be about war.

Maybe it would be   if I had not found   the photo this way
and the world was safer   for you   without me
when I left it behind.

THREE GIRLS TALKING ABOUT LOVE

Suddenly, they are sullen,
laughter gone,
eyes focused
on dark brown coffee.

Love has knotted their wills:
elusive, warring,
filling their beautiful voices
with scars.

ALL THAT REMAINS

Sweeping around the radiator
is how I find them—

two large shards
of the glass I slammed to the floor,

frustrated by all
we could not say.

The cup shattered on impact,
large plastic wedges sliding across the floor.

I thought I had retrieved them all
as you stormed out, adding to the hole we had yet to fill.

This morning's light shines just where they sit,
exposing these ruins of our death that day,

the dust of the earth resting heavy
on their withered bodies

as if the earth, too, refused
to hold out for one last idyll of hope,

its wounds weeping, its flesh pushing
these last visceral reminders into the light.

I bend to sweep them up
with the dust and debris,

each piece rattling in the pan
before falling into the trash beneath the sink,

before they are carried to the bin
behind the house

where they will be carried away
to the landfill at the edge of town

with the other shards of pasts,
which have already been forgotten.

ON A NIGHT NOT UNLIKE ANY OTHER

We have not spoken a word since you handed me your scissors.
There's no other way you said as you laid the silver blades across
my palm. When you said it, I knew you meant the wine.
But after chipping and chipping the cork away slowly,
we both know there's another reason this is hard.
His picture is framed on your bedside table.

We will grieve when this is done, the new light of morning
resting on our faces, our bodies beneath the sheets
where it will still be warm despite the heavy rains
which, in the night, will tip the last glass of wine
onto the window sill. A pool of blood. That, as of now,
trapped inside this bottle, still belongs to me.

With one final punch, the cork pushes down into the red sea,
splashes us both just a little with wine, with laughter—the first
since we sat down on your bed, eyes focused on each other
like birds of prey diving quietly into tall grass
to take what they need most of all from this earth, to carry it back
into the air, racing toward the sun, as if toward their god
who refuses to be kept in waiting.

MAKING HISTORY

We have already begun the task of naming
what is yours and what is mine. Even now,
walking through the apartment alone, I am
making lists of what I will ask to have,
to take with me:
                              your bare feet lifting and settling
on polished hardwood floors with a faint, faint
padding I will leave behind.

The voice of the woman next door rises up
through the trees by the kitchen window.
I stop to listen, my coffee cooling in the morning breeze
that carries with it the first sign that summer is coming
to an end.

She is singing an old, Russian folk-song, a song
her husband used to sing when he worked in the yard.
I know this because she told me. She can't work without
singing it now. She used to sing along with him, in the house
under her breath, never realizing she was until each time
he found her sweeping or dusting and singing.

I imagine he would stand there first, silently, watching
and listening the way a man does when he catches his wife
alone, engrossed in the tiny details of her love for him.

He passed away before I met him. And maybe I am wrong,
but she seems happiest this way, working the way he did,
as if telling his story day after day, alone in the yard
her voice carrying up from the flowerbeds over the fences
to where I stand, back to the window, humming along.

I will, no doubt, take this with me. This moment. Her voice.
Perhaps I will pass it on. Or, perhaps it will die with me,
coming to pass in a place far from home, a quiet safe place
which will have no history, like you and me.

NOTES AND REFERENCES

Epigraphs: taken from Adrienne Rich's "A long Conversation" in *Midnight Salvage* (New York and London: W. W. Norton & Company, 1999); Adrienne Rich's "Diving Into The Wreck" in *Diving Into The Wreck* (New York and London: W. W. Norton & Company, 1973); Larry Levis's "Elegy With an Angel at Its Gates" in *Elegy* (Pittsburgh: University of Pittsburgh Press, 1997).

"Elegy to Young Boys Jumping off the End of the Dock"; "Elegy to the Heart and All That It Endures": both poems written to honor the spirit of Larry Levis's *Elegy* (Pittsburgh: University of Pittsburgh Press, 1997).

"Proving Grounds": the last line is derived from the last two lines of Lisel Mueller's "Blood Oranges" in *Second Language* (Baton Rouge and London: Louisiana State University Press, 1986).

"Toward Some Provincial Heaven": the poem is based on one of 144 photographs displayed in windows of cooperative retail and residential establishments along Lake Street in "Uptown" Minneapolis, Minnesota. The artist was Wing Young Huie. The display was titled, "Lake Street USA."

"Under the Missing and Innumerable Stars": the title is taken from the last line of Larry Levis's "Anastastasia and Sandman" in *Elegy* (Pittsburgh: University of Pittsburgh Press, 1977); "at what could have been either the beginning/ or the end of the world" derived from Carolyn Forche's "Ourselves or Nothing" in *The Country Between Us* (New York: Harper & Row, Publishers, 1981).

"Endurance": "to forgive each other of our deepest sadness" derived from Lisel Mueller's "Necessities" in *Second Language* (Baton Rouge and London: Louisiana State University Press, 1986).

"Mothers and Sons": the story of the woman who perished while climbing is derived from Adrienne Rich's "Phantasia for Elvira

Shatayve" in *The Dream of A Common Language* (New York and London: W. W. Norton & Company, 1978).

ABOUT THE AUTHOR

Ralph Pennel is the author of *A World Less Perfect for Dying In*, (by Červená Barva Press, 2015). His writing has appeared in *The Cape Rock*, *Ropes*, *Open to Interpretation*, *Ibbetson Street*, *The Smoking Poet*, *Unbound Press*, *Monologues From the Road* and various other journals in the U.S. and abroad. Ralph teaches poetry at Bentley University and literature at Bunker Hill Community College. He has been a guest lecturer at Emerson College and served as the judge for the 2013 WLP Dean's Prize for Emerson. Ralph also teaches workshops at the Cambridge Center for Adult Education and for Student Day of Poetry run by MassPoetry.org. He is a founding editor and the fiction editor for the online literary magazine, *Midway Journal* (www.midwayjournal.com), published out of St. Paul, Minnesota. Ralph Pennel lives and writes in Somerville, Massachusetts, and was a finalist for the Poet Laureate of Somerville in 2014.